GOVERNMENT
BY
DECREE

From President to Dictator through Executive Orders

D1413211

James L. Hirsen

Huntington House Publishers

Huntington House Publishers
P.O. Box 53788
Lafayette, Louisiana 70505

Library of Congress Card Catalog
Number 99-70835
ISBN 1-56384-166-5

Introduction

The American spirit embodies many intangible ideals—freedom, justice, equality, fairness, respect. As children, we drink in the meaning of these words. As adults, we cherish the value of their expression in motion. These qualities are not merely clichés, but rather they are hallmarks of virtue, reflecting the uniqueness of the country in which we live.

Yet, as is the nature of humankind, complacency comes so easily. The unpleasant realities of history are readily forgotten. The fragile nature of our unrivaled system of government does not linger within our collective consciousness.

Imagine for a moment that you are relaxing in your own home. Suddenly you hear a knock on the door. When you answer, you are immediately grabbed, ripped from your home, stripped of your private property, and carried away against your will to a concentration camp where you are held prisoner. Where could something so awful as this happen? Nazi Germany? The old Soviet Union? Cuba? Probably, but this happened in 1942 to some 100,000 people in our own country. The whole thing occurred without public debate or approval from Congress. A simple signature was all that was needed to create such powerful and life-changing consequences for American citizens. President Franklin Delano Roosevelt provided his name. The instrument he used to unilaterally create law is called an executive order.

The founding fathers of this nation established a republic, with a highly effective system of checks and balances, precisely because they wanted to avoid, at all costs, the concentration of power in any one person. Our young country had just broken away from an oppressive ruler, and as a people, we had a deep desire to prevent any future dictator from emerging. When a president creates new law through executive order, this carefully crafted mode of representative government is literally evaded. The notion of separation of powers is no longer a part of the legislative process.

The presidential executive order was, at one time, a genuine exercise of power, based upon law that already existed. Unfortunately, it has been distorted into a tool for the wrongful creation of new law. This violates both the spirit and the letter of the Constitution. The practice has been tolerated by Congress and, occasionally, even concealed from the public, all for the sake of getting a job done swiftly and without interference.

The Formation of an Imperial Presidency

"Stroke of a pen. Law of the land. Kind of cool."[1]

The flippant tone of Paul Begala, a White House adviser, came through loud and clear in his statement. His uttering of the description above reflected the Clinton administration's view of the unilateral creation of law through the use of executive orders. Begala was referring to the habit of modern presidents, in particular, President Bill Clinton, to create law by signing a document, with no input from Congress, and many times without informing the public until after the fact.

This is law by fiat, pure and simple. Throughout history, corrupt monarchs and depraved dictators have used this approach of legislation by decree. Taxes were raised to exorbitant levels. Burdensome regulations were imposed on the people through pronouncements or edicts given from those wielding authority. Citizens were often deprived of their very livelihoods. What is relevant for us today, and important for every citizen to know, is that executive orders vest the power of a monarch on whoever happens to hold the office of the presidency.

How did the presidency ever acquire a mechanism that allows laws to be made without the normal constitutional protections of representative government? To answer this question, we must look to the origin of this distinctive power.

It is somewhat difficult to know exactly how many executive orders have been issued throughout our country's history, because prior to 1907, executive orders were not numbered. Beginning in that year, a number was assigned to each executive order, and the orders were filed chronologically by the State Department. Estimates of unnumbered executive orders range from fifteen thousand to as high as fifty thousand.[2] Today, executive orders contain up to five digits, and since 1907 over thirteen thousand have been issued.

The Constitution designates Congress as the branch of government with the exclusive function of lawmaking. It is the job of the executive branch to carry out the laws that Congress makes. Consistent with this balance, executive orders and other forms of presidential directives were intended by our forefathers to be communications to various divisions of the executive branch of the federal government, based upon existing authority under established law. This means, when functioning properly, an executive order is a directive that should communicate and carry out legitimate executive power. Routine executive orders deal with government agencies and officials. They establish governmental bureaus, modify rules, change procedures, and enforce existing statutes. Examples of the appropriate exercise of authority through executive orders include establishing rules for executive branch employees, authorizing agency policies, granting presidential awards, and putting forth commands to cabinet officers.

Beyond the Limits of Power

Despite the original intent of the Constitution, presidents have tested the constitutional envelope of this power throughout our country's history. Even presidents who were more aggressive in asserting power indicated that they were limited by the Constitution and other federal laws. This thinking was expressed forcefully by one irrepressible believer in an expansive presidency, President Teddy Roosevelt, when he said:

> I did and caused to be done many things not previously done by the president and the heads of the departments. I did not usurp power, but I did greatly broaden the use of executive power. In other words, I acted for the public welfare, I acted for the common well being of all our people,

whenever and in whatever manner was necessary, unless prevented by direct constitutional or legislative prohibition.[3]

A more cautious view was maintained by his successor to the presidency, President William Howard Taft:

The true view of the exclusive functions is, as I can see that, that the President can exercise no power which can not be fairly and reasonably traced to some specific grant of power or justly implied and included within such express grant as proper and necessary to its exercise. Such specific grant must be either in the federal constitution or in an act of congress passed in pursuance thereof. There is no undefined residuum of power, which he can exercise because it seems to him to be in the public interest, . . . [his] jurisdiction must be justified and vindicated by affirmative constitutional or statutory provision, or it does not exist.[4]

Wellsprings of Subversion

The fact that Congress and the public seem to favor giving the president more leeway when it comes to dealing with national security, international affairs, and, most recently, economic issues may explain why presidential power has expanded over the years. This expansion of presidential power really accelerated under President Franklin Roosevelt's New Deal. The economic crisis of the Great Depression gave Roosevelt wide latitude in instituting initiatives. In 1943 Roosevelt issued 654 executive orders.[5] This is in stark contrast with presidents who used these instruments to perform routine, non-lawmaking functions. Grover Cleveland issued only 71 executive orders and William McKinley issued just 51.

Roosevelt used his executive order power to act quickly, since he had to deal with the banking system and the creation of various new agencies. One of Roosevelt's most controversial executive orders, and quite frankly, a blot on modern American history, was Executive Order 9066. This unfortunate presidential initiative actually was rooted in a prevailing attitude of paranoia. It resulted in the movement of Americans of Japanese descent from the West Coast to confinement in detention camps in the southwestern desert. Astoundingly, this form of imprisonment lasted for the duration of World War II.[6] This all happened in 1942—not that long ago. To compound the assault on the civil liberties of these maligned U.S. citizens, citizens of German and Italian descent were not treated in this same manner. The Supreme Court in 1944 placed the legal stamp of authenticity on Roosevelt's action.[7] The Court reasoned that a military necessity existed. The Court cited evidence of disloyalty on the part of some individuals and acknowledged that military authorities had only a short time to act.[8]

Roosevelt abandoned any pretense of tying the executive order power to existing law. He claimed to derive "general powers" because of the position of the presidency. In June 1941 Roosevelt decided to take control of a California manufacturing plant, which was owned by North American Aviation. He used an executive order to accomplish this task. There was no existing statute to use as a basis for the executive order, so President Roosevelt justified his move by citing the general powers of the office that he held.[9] When Roosevelt seized shipbuilding companies, a shell plant, almost 4,000 coal companies, and a cable company in the same year, he invoked these general powers once again.[10]

In 1952 during the Korean War, President Harry S. Truman ordered a federal seizure of the country's steel mills to end a labor management dispute. The courts later invalidated his actions.[11] The judiciary struck down President Truman's attempt to take over the steel mills of the nation because it was not justified by either an existing statute or by the Constitution.[12] The Supreme Court reasoned that it is the president's job to see that the laws are faithfully executed. This duty refutes the idea that the president should be a lawmaker.[13] In a terse statement, the High Court confirmed that having the people's representatives make laws is part of the original intent of the Constitution. "The Founders of this Nation entrusted the lawmaking powers to the Congress alone in both good and bad times."[14]

In 1950 President Truman established the Subversive Activities Control Board (SACB), ostensibly to investigate Communist activities. All Communist organizations had to register with the board under the terms of the executive order. Again the courts spoke on the validity of these executive orders and held that this registration violated the

Constitution's Fifth Amendment privilege against self-incrimination.[15] Still, the SACB was given new life in 1971 through an executive order signed by President Richard M. Nixon, expanding the board's jurisdiction.[16]

In 1971 President Nixon, through the use of a proclamation, added a 10 percent surcharge on imports as part of an economic policy.[17] President Gerald R. Ford did the same with a proclamation on imported oil, and in 1980 President Jimmy Carter also used a proclamation to implement a fee on oil imports. For some reason the courts upheld the maneuvers of Nixon and Ford but overturned the action of Jimmy Carter.[18]

When civil rights took on a more primary role in society, anti-discrimination initiatives were produced, once again through the use of executive orders. President Franklin D. Roosevelt signed an executive order that prohibited discrimination toward workers in defense industries or government. President John F. Kennedy threatened to cancel defense contracts in order to enforce federal equal employment standards. In addition, President Lyndon B. Johnson issued an executive order that created an administrative body for carrying out this non-discrimination policy.[19]

Although executive orders have some constitutionally legitimate purposes, they have been increasingly used in an unauthorized manner. Despite some benefits that may occur as a result of their use, this expanding power of the presidency poses a serious danger to the essential divisions between the three branches of government that preserve the republic.

Judicial Surrender

These various rules and regulations that are issued by presidents have been ruled by the United States Supreme Court to be binding as long as they are within the sphere of legal and constitutional authority.[20] Under the Constitution, Congress has the exclusive power to make laws. The Constitution states with respect to laws that the president has the power to "take Care that the Laws be faithfully executed."[21] However, this power has grown to include a wide variety of *implied* powers. These implied powers have moved well beyond anything the founding fathers would have contemplated.[22]

American history has seen a pattern of struggle with presidents attempting to exercise power beyond the Constitution. Reading the express language of the Constitution, the president's job is to administer the law in accordance with Congress's intent. This power has been expanded beyond the area of passed legislation to a broad and nebulous grant of power. In the case of *In re Neagle* (1890), the Supreme Court said that the president was not limited to laws that had been passed by Congress, but the president could administer laws based on those growing out of the Constitution itself, international relations, and "all the protection implied by the nature of the government under the Constitution."[23]

It is this kind of language that has allowed the president to assert power well beyond what is set forth in the Constitution. These implied powers gave birth to the modern day executive order, the ultimate conduit of presidential power.

National Insecurity

Historically, when it comes to matters of national security, broader presidential discretion has been granted. It is generally understood that a balance between guarding the nation from enemies abroad and protecting citizens from abuses of power must be maintained for continuity within the American system.

Presidential secrecy has often been described as a vital part of national security. No doubt, at critical moments, the president has a need to safeguard "military, diplomatic or sensitive national security secrets."[24] However, national security is a particularly troubling area when it involves the use of executive orders to classify government documents as "secret." The difficulty arises when we ask the crucial question: What must be classified as secret? Since in national security issues, the president is given more power, secret is apparently whatever the president, acting as commander-in-chief, believes would be harmful to the nation's defense.[25] Such a presidential act did not occur until 1940, when President Franklin Roosevelt authorized classification of military intelligence information during World War II.

In 1972 the *New York Times* published the *Pentagon Papers,* the Defense Department's top-secret study of the growth of United States military involvement in Vietnam. President Nixon issued an executive order, which defined national security, for classification purposes, as any information "in the interest of the national defense or foreign relations of the United States."[26] Nixon included information about domestic intelligence in his application of this definition. The Department of Justice had asked for a temporary restraining order, which was granted. This provided the Supreme Court with an opportunity to determine whether the First Amendment right of freedom of the press, in this case, would allow the publication of matters that the executive branch had classified as secret for national security. The High Court ruled in the newspaper's favor, allowing the *Pentagon Papers* to be published.[27]

The idea of having the power of lawmaking consolidated in the hands of one individual is disconcerting in and of itself. When this authority can be exercised in secret, the inherent dangers become greatly magnified.

Ripe for Abuse

When presidents exercise this kind of power, unrestrained by the Constitution or congressional legislation, and unaccountable to congressional oversight, the possibility for abuse hovers. If related activities can be conducted in secret by using a national security classification, the potential for abuse rises significantly.

In 1971 President Nixon issued Executive Order 11605. This created a new authority for the executive branch to investigate individual Americans, seemingly to discover whether they constituted a threat to the security of the nation. Activities that were sanctioned in carrying out this executive order included secret wire tapping, breaking into offices, and utilizing undercover informants to infiltrate suspicious groups.

President Ronald Reagan's executive order of September 1986, which authorized arms shipments to Iran, was a classified order and therefore not known to the public. President Reagan had a good reason for this classification. He had to postpone notification of the order. If information had leaked out, harm could have come to the hostages that were being held in Lebanon by groups closely tied with Iran. Still, this situation illustrates the breadth of this presidential prerogative.

Executive orders tend to build upon each other, with previous orders justifying subsequent ones. This has happened most notably in the civil rights area. The executive orders in question are issued over and over again, and the courts tend to legitimize them, when in reality they are inconsistent with the doctrine of separation of powers contained in our Constitution. Wrongs are compounded when previous illegitimately issued executive orders are relied upon as lawful justification for subsequent executive orders.

The problem with governing by decree is that public accountability is not a part of the equation. Because law, in essence, can be made at will, and sometimes in secret, both Congress and the public are excluded from the entire legislative process.

In Case of Emergency— Exert Control

As previously noted, the genesis of the expansion of discretionary powers of the presidency was due to the onset of a crisis. One of the most menacing components of governmental power expansion is the use of so-called emergency powers. The reason that emergency powers are dangerous is that they can undermine the very safeguards that the founding fathers placed within our form of government. Our system is designed to split power to protect the rights of the states and the people. The most obvious national emergency situation involves war, but other domestic and international crises, real and questionable, have come into play to justify the use of executive orders.

In 1971 Richard Nixon declared an emergency because of the growing discrepancy in our federal balance of payments. He disconnected the value of the dollar from the gold standard, levied a surtax on imports, and froze domestic prices for ninety days. Many people thought Nixon was overreacting to the circumstances at hand, but regardless of which opinion dominated the discussion, the situation clearly showed a president stretching beyond the boundaries of constitutional power.

Historical precedent also exists for use of presidential emergency powers when dealing with domestic unrest. Presidents used troops to desegregate the public schools during the 1960s. Presidential action is, of course, justified in certain emergencies, especially when natural disasters such as earthquakes, floods, and hurricanes strike.

In an inauspicious move on 3 June 1994, President Bill Clinton issued an executive order that consolidated a number of prior executive orders issued by his predecessors in the White House.[28] Originally created in 1962 by President John F. Kennedy, this particular collection of executive orders reveals a frightening interference with many of the freedoms that Americans generally take for granted. The first of the Kennedy-issued executive orders allows the president to take control of all media for as long as a national emergency exists. Included as media are radio, television, and, conceivably, telephone and internet outlets.[29] Another executive order from this cluster allows the seizure of all facilities that produce energy, including electricity, gasoline, and solid fuels.[30]

Disturbingly, what can be labeled as a national emergency has not yet been clearly defined by the courts. Rather than setting forth specific criteria, the courts have given the president sweeping and expansive discretion to determine the boundaries of what constitutes a national emergency. The familiar rationale is that the president should be given extra room to maneuver during emergencies due to the need for swift action.[31] Evidently, in the event of a crisis situation, our food resources could be taken over by the executive branch. This would presumably include all agriculture, distribution, and retail facilities.[32] All means of transportation, both public and private, including ground and air transportation, could be completely controlled by the executive branch as well.[33] In a reprise of the Japanese internment, another executive order allows for the involuntary relocation of workers. The order also grants the executive branch authority to take over labor, services, and manpower resources.[34]

In 1933 the U.S. Congress passed the War and Emergency Powers Act, and it has never been repealed. These powers are centered in an agency of the federal government known as the Federal Emergency Management Agency (FEMA). In fact,

FEMA itself came into existence under an executive order.[35] An emergency is defined by federal law as follows: "Emergency means any occasion or instance for which, in the determination of the President, federal assistance is needed to supplement state and local efforts and capabilities to save lives and to protect property and public health and safety, or to lessen or avert the threat of a catastrophe in any part of the United States."[36] What the War and Emergency Powers Act does, in conjunction with the above-mentioned executive orders, is enable the president to suspend the Constitution at will. All that the president needs to take this type of action is a national emergency.

Bill Clinton and the Executive Order

In actuality, President Clinton had his eye fixed upon the executive order power from the beginning of his presidency. In fact, after Bill Clinton was elected, the issuance of an executive order was one of his first official acts. On 22 January 1993 the president signed an executive order that ended a gag rule that had been in force under both the Reagan and Bush administrations. The gag rule had prohibited abortion counseling and referrals from taking place at family planning clinics that received federal funding.

However, a turning point was reached in 1994 when the Democrats lost control of the House of Representatives. As a result, the ability of President Clinton to initiate policy became noticeably more restricted. Beset by a series of scandals and faced with an adversarial Congress, he sought another way to promote his policies. Thus, through-

out his term, President Clinton used executive
orders, regulations, proclamations, and other forms
of presidential memoranda to circumvent Congress.

A crucial executive order, Presidential Decision Directive 25 (P.D.D. 25), was executed by
President Clinton in 1994. The State Department
released a summary of the directive, but the details
of P.D.D. 25 remain classified to this very day.
Nevertheless, the summary does indicate that the
president has the power to place U.S. armed forces
under foreign command. There seemed to be an
effort, however, to convey the information in a
subdued fashion, so that the concept was more
palatable, as the following excerpt demonstrates:

> Defining clearly our policy regarding the
> command and control of American mili-
> tary forces in U.N. peace operations. The
> policy directive underscores the fact that
> the President will never relinquish com-
> mand of U.S. forces. However, as Com-
> mander-in-Chief, the President has the au-
> thority to place U.S. forces under the op-
> erational control of a foreign commander
> when doing so serves American security
> interests, just as American leaders have
> done numerous times since the Revolu-
> tionary War, including in Operation Desert
> Storm. The greater the anticipated U.S.
> military role, the less likely it will be that
> the U.S. will agree to have a U.N. com-
> mander exercise overall operational control
> over U.S. forces.[37]

This executive order actually authorizes the president to place United States military forces under the control of a foreign commander. Not surprisingly, it did not take long for this authority to be exploited. During the Clinton administration, U.S. military forces participated in a number of United Nations interventionist efforts, including actions in Somalia, Macedonia, and Haiti.

Some interesting research was conducted prior to the signing of P.D.D. 25. A Combat Arms Survey was distributed to a group of U.S. Marines, which asked, among other things, whether the participants would be willing to fire on U.S. citizens. One of the true or false hypotheticals read as follows:

> The U.S. government declares a ban on the possession, sale, transportation, and transfer of all non-sporting firearms. A thirty (30) day amnesty period is permitted for these firearms to be turned over to the local authorities. At the end of this period, a number of citizen groups refuse to turn over their firearms. Consider the following statement: I would fire upon U.S. citizens who refuse or resist confiscation of firearms banned by the U.S. government.[38]

Every American upon learning this information should be asking why members of the United States military would ever be questioned as to their willingness to use force against their own citizens. The reasonable assumption is an alarming one. It is quite possible that this option has already been discussed, and perhaps our own government officials have even given some legitimate consideration to the notion. Louis Fisher, an expert on constitutional law, has stated that Bill Clinton has "an expansive view of presidential power over military initiatives." Fisher also stated, "Mr. Clinton's interpretation of the presidential war power would have astonished the framers of the Constitution."[39]

In another use of executive orders, President Clinton authorized the Food and Drug Administration in 1995 to declare nicotine an addictive drug. This act cleared the way for an attack on the tobacco industry. The White House had suggested that the president was trying to deal with a serious problem that the Congress had failed to address. In reality, President Clinton was once again legislating from the executive branch. Jeremy Taylor, a director of natural resource studies at the Cato Institute, stated, "This president distinguishes himself from past presidents by the aggressiveness with which he has expanded his authority without explicit congressional approval."[40]

In 1995, over the objections of Congress, President Clinton tapped a special treasury fund to bail out the Mexican economy. In the same year, President Clinton also issued an executive order that barred federal agencies from signing contracts with companies that permanently replaced striking workers. However, this order was struck down by the U.S. Court of Appeals for the District of Columbia because it had been made in violation of the National Labor Relations Act.

In July of 1998 William Jefferson Clinton returned from a highly publicized trip to China.

With the cloud of the Monica Lewinsky investigation hanging over his head and a Republican-controlled Congress in place, President Clinton's agenda did not look altogether promising, so he decided to focus his energies on two main areas. The first focal point involved his penchant for fundraising, in which he continued to engage despite lingering questions about the 1996 presidential campaign. The second area to receive attention was equally brazen. Clinton would take aggressive lawmaking action, but he would not do this in the conventional way. He was determined to avoid the burdens of the legislative process. Instead, he was going to accomplish legislation through the increased application of executive orders.[41] President Clinton immediately announced new regulations to increase the safety of fruit and vegetable juices. He stated further that he planned to issue a series of executive orders to demonstrate his effectiveness and to show the country that he was not a lame duck.[42] Following the recommendation of his former adviser, Dick Morris, President Clinton set out to flood Washington with an additional series of incremental executive orders.

Legacy of Presidential Misappropriation

President Clinton's interest in executive orders extended beyond the mere furtherance of his agenda. Rather, he had a long history of desiring to manipulate the media for political purposes.

In February of 1997 when a patient's bill of rights was created for all federal health plans, the media was inundated with heart-rending stories from "victims" of the health care system. This enabled the Democratic party to place political pressure on Republicans to pass legislation with similar provisions.

Under guidance from former adviser Dick Morris, President Clinton used executive orders to enact a number of small, focus group-researched initiatives. He proceeded to glut the wire services with news of his accomplishments. For example, after the first sheep was cloned, President Clinton issued an executive order banning the use of federal funds for human cloning. In addition, he issued an executive order mandating the use of child safety locks on guns for all federal law enforcement officers. Even though such actions had a minimal effect, President Clinton was able to successfully manipulate the media, and likewise the public, into believing otherwise.[43] Elizabeth Shoburn of the *Los Angeles Times* reported that Clinton has "rewritten the manual on how to use executive powers, some professors and analysts argue. His formula includes pressing the limits of his regulatory authority, signing executive orders and using other unilateral means to obtain his policy priorities when Congress fails to embrace them."[44]

It is not simply the number of executive orders President Clinton issued that is disturbing, but the nature of the orders that lends to the gravity of his actions. He was resolute in his desire to encroach upon the legislative function. In this way, he was able to enhance his image by appearing engaged, despite the fact that he was unable to successfully prevail upon Congress to pass his desired legislative initiatives.[45] White House adviser Paul Begala commented on President Clinton's inclination for bypassing Congress saying, "This President has a very strong sense of the powers of the presidency and is willing to use all of them."[46] Although other presidents have used executive authority to promote and to achieve their policy goals, President Clinton discarded the ground rules when it came to the use of executive powers.[47]

Good-bye, Tenth Amendment

Part of the pattern in Clinton's executive order practice seems to reflect a desire to overturn executive orders that had been implemented by President Ronald Reagan. President Reagan had issued Executive Order 12606, which was intended to protect the family. President Clinton revoked this order by Executive Order 13045. President Reagan's Executive Order 12291 requiring all federal rules to have a cost-benefit analysis was revoked by President Clinton's Executive Order 12866.

The most serious blow yet to the Constitution, though, occurred on 14 May 1998. Without any announcement, President Clinton's White House released a new executive order dealing with the subject of federalism. Federalism refers to the scope and classification of power that resides in the states as opposed to the federal government. While in Birmingham, England, President Clinton signed Executive Order 13083. This revoked Executive Order 12612 that was issued by President Reagan in 1987. However, Executive Order 13083 did more than just cancel Ronald Reagan's policy on federalism. It struck at the very constitutional foundations of the relationship of the federal government, state governments, and the people. In effect, it voided the language of the Tenth Amendment of the Bill of Rights,[48] which reads: "The powers not delegated to the United States by the Constitution, nor prohibited by it to the states, are reserved to the states respectively, or to the people."[49]

This new executive order set forth various reasons to justify federal action that could directly interfere with state sovereignty, such as an increase in the cost of government resulting from decentralization. Any federal initiative could theoretically be deemed legitimate by saying that it would simply cost too much to delegate or to allow such power to remain with the states. States are usually reluctant to impose unnecessary regulations on their local economies, fearing business relocation, job loss, and detriment to the communities. However, the federal government does not have such concerns. One of the criteria from Executive Order 13083 states that federal action is justified whenever there is a "need for uniform national standards."[50] Who decides when such a need exists? The executive branch of the federal government no doubt will oblige. Similarly, under this order the federal government is given carte blanche to invade state sovereignty when "States have not adequately protected individual rights and liberties."[51] Even the states' economy and standard of living must not stand in the way of this federal juggernaut. The order dictates that if the citizens of a particular state find themselves "reluctant to impose necessary regulations because of fears that business activity will relocate to other States,"[52] this will not impede federal action. These criteria basically say that the federal government can interfere in the sovereignty of the states however and whenever it so wishes. This type of rationale undermines everything for which the Constitution and the Bill of Rights stand. There is no legitimate justification under constitutional law, either historically or through precedence, for this kind of power grab.[53]

An Attempt Thwarted?

Two months after President Clinton signed Executive Order 13083, representatives of state and local governments had what the *Washington Post* described as a "stormy meeting" with the chief of White House intergovernmental relations, Mickey Ibarra.[54] The reason this meeting was held was because no state or local government official was consulted or informed in any way regarding the drafting of such a pervasive executive order, an order that attacked the very essence of constitutional federalism. The representatives that came to the meeting drafted a letter to President Clinton and demanded that he withdraw the executive order. The letter stated: "We are concerned that all references to the Tenth Amendment, identification of new costs or burdens, preemption and reduction of unfunded mandates are revoked . . . we believe the changes in the order in the manner in which they were made raise serious questions about the administration's commitment to partnership with state and local governments.[55]

On 5 August 1998 President Clinton, under pressure from governors, mayors, and members of Congress, suspended Executive Order 13083 by issuing Executive Order 13095. To punctuate the matter, the House voted to nullify the same executive order on the very same day. Organizations pressuring Clinton to suspend the order were the National Council of State Legislatures, the Council of States Governments, the National Association of Counties, the U.S. Conference of Mayors, the National League of Cities, and the International Cities/County Management Association.[56]

Despite the suspension of the order by President Clinton, a problem still remains. Executive Order 13083 revoked President Reagan's Executive Order 12612. President Reagan's order had strengthened the power of states to deal with the growth of federal power. Executive Order 13095, the order that suspended 13083, does not reinstate President Reagan's original Executive Order 12612. Moreover, President Clinton's Executive Order 13095 is not a revocation, but merely a suspension. The Congress, governors, mayors, and the American people should not be lulled into a false sense of security over the suspension, for this executive order might someday rear its ugly head again, and a federal power grab may be tried once more.

White House spokesman Barry Toiv said, "We want to sit down with representatives of state and local governments, and we hope to get this done by the fall."[57] When asked how this executive order had been signed without any input, notice, or consultation with state and local officials, Toiv commented, "This just slipped through the cracks."[58]

Confiscation by the Commander-in-Chief

Executive orders can produce a powerful attack on private property rights. A number of programs forwarded by the Clinton administration illustrate such an assault.

In 1996 there was an attempt to pass the Heritage Areas Act in Congress, but the effort went down to defeat. Under the original act, Congress would have had the authority to designate areas of land as heritage zones. Undeterred by the failed passage, the Clinton administration simply repackaged the act and issued it as an executive order. On 11 September 1997 President Clinton issued Executive Order 13061, which "officially" established the American Heritage Rivers Initiative (AHRI).[59] Its purpose was ostensibly to provide federal assistance to local communities in order to protect the environment, preserve waterfronts, and conserve local history. In actuality, the AHRI was a way for the federal government to take control over large parcels of land adjacent to U.S. rivers.

The waters within the border of a state had been, up to this time, the exclusive province of state sovereignty. Now, however, as a result of the AHRI, local communities within proximity to a river that is designated as an "American Heritage

Site" become eligible for federal money and other benefits. The program initially involved ten rivers, but the plan is to continuously add rivers over time. In July 1998 fourteen new rivers were added to the original ten.[60] Rules governing each river system are administered by a presidentially-appointed bureaucrat. The President's Council on Environmental Quality oversees the entire scheme. Each year, additional rivers will be selected for inclusion by the presiding president. Eventually, over one hundred rivers will be added. Needless to say, owners of private property along the riverbanks are the most likely to suffer adverse consequences when rivers are designated and the AHRI is fully implemented.

This initiative was instigated in a swift yet quiet manner, and it was executed without the appropriate congressional approval. The Clinton administration chose to act as a legislature and basically ignore the Constitution. Although the AHRI, like so many other proposals, may sound virtuous, the underlying motives are quite sinister. For all practical purposes, the executive order for the AHRI is an unconstitutional transfer of power from the states to the federal government.[61] Idaho Congresswoman Helen Chenoweth stated, "Its purpose was . . . a federal land grab, or a federal takeover of power that rightfully belongs to the states.[62]

In another egregious assault on state sovereignty, President Clinton took a step that enraged Congress, the public, and the government of the state of Utah. The president declared that nearly two million acres of Utah land would thereafter be considered a national monument. This huge land transfer did not occur as the result of representative government in action, nor was it the consequence of any congressional effort. It all happened by means of an executive order. Again, just one signature was required. The land was literally snatched away from the people of the state of Utah. To compound matters, hundreds of thousands of acres of private land were also seized. It turned out that this was a grandstanding effort on the part of President Clinton to win additional favor with environmental constituents, since the designation as a national monument would prohibit mining of the land. This meant that one of the greatest untapped natural resources in the United States, which included tens of billions of tons of high quality coal, trillions of cubic feet of natural gas, three million tons of zirconium and titanium, and billions of barrels of oil, would go untouched. The people of Utah were not even informed of the decision that had been made prior to its announcement. The executive order that made the Utah land a national monument was described by Utah Republican Congressman James Hansen in the following way: "The manner in which the White House hid this decision from the people of Utah . . . displays an alarming disregard for the Constitution."[63]

Executive Orders:
Tool of the International Agenda

The United Nations has a program which earmarks certain places around the globe for special protection. Such areas are designated as World Heritage Sites. In the United States, Yellowstone National Park has been given this special status. Yellowstone National Park is made up of over 2.2 million acres of land. Because it has been selected as a World Heritage Site, it falls under the jurisdiction of the United Nations. The park has what is known as a "buffer zone" around it, which is additional land that is highly regulated in the name of environmental protection. The World Heritage Program has specific language in its operating guidelines to ensure that buffer zones are free from "human encroachment." The buffer zone could someday include other parts of the states of Wyoming, Utah, Idaho, and Montana. Over 15 million acres of public and private land could ultimately be affected.

The Crown Butte New World Gold Mine of Wyoming is located five miles outside of Yellowstone. According to the United Nations, the gold mine is situated too close to Yellowstone National Park and intrudes upon the buffer zone, so in 1995 the mine was shut down. Despite the fact that no environmental problems had been reported to any state agency, UNESCO officials wanted to close the mine so that the UN could exert control over a greater amount of territory. The Clinton administration aligned itself with the United Nations and supported the closure of the gold mine. In this case, international law, implemented by the executive branch, was used to usurp both federal and state sovereignty. Private property ownership suffered tremendous violation yet again.

Once land has been marked as a World Heritage Site, international environmentalists join forces with domestic environmentalists to accomplish their mutual goals. One technique used repeatedly, and with surprising success, is to attack the rights of landowners surrounding a World Heritage Site. For instance, in 1993 the World Heritage Committee recognized Everglades National Park as a World Heritage Site. Farmers whose land was located north of the park were barraged with new restrictions, regulations, and land use laws. The new rules had a devastating impact on the agricultural industry in the affected areas.

When Unratified Treaties Become Law

Treaties, in and of themselves, are a latent threat to representative government because they have the potential to override both state and federal laws.[64] Treaties are required by the Constitution to be ratified by a two-thirds vote of the Senate before they become the law of the land. Executive orders are a way to further the content of international treaties without ratification.

Behind many of the current international initiatives is a sweeping plan to control the majority of the United States using environmentalism as a pretext. The intention is to eventually institute an international agenda, but in order to be successful, the necessary elements must be put in place gradually. First, the president must sign the intended treaty on behalf of the nation. Then, the treaty in question must be ratified by the U.S. Senate. If ratification fails, it is attempted again and again,

and, in the meantime, implementation is sought
in piecemeal fashion through other avenues.

In the case of the Biodiversity Treaty, which
was an international incursion that came out of
the Rio Earth Summit in 1992, President Clinton
took the first step of signing the treaty in 1993.
The Senate rejected the treaty, pursuant to its constitutional approval power. The Clinton administration, though, made it clear that ratification
would remain a prime objective until success was
achieved. Singular provisions of the treaty were
then implemented in incremental steps through
executive orders and memoranda.

The Global Biodiversity Assessment (GBA)[65]
is the implementing language of the Biodiversity
Treaty. Hidden behind high-minded terms such
as buffer zones, corridors, and core reserves lies a
philosophy that relegates human needs to a level
below those of other life forms. The GBA trans-
forms the way land use would be regulated by
establishing commissions, administered by the government and affiliated with the UN, to control
property usage. If this project were to take full
effect, human activity would literally be reduced
throughout the entire country. Approximately a
quarter of the land in the continental United States
would be set aside as wilderness area.[66] Also included in the GBA is a plan to relocate citizens
over a period of twenty to fifty years, so that people
are completely removed from so-called environ-
mentally sensitive areas.[67] Needless to say, if citizens are relocated to "approved areas," industry,
farming, forestry, mining, and other commercial
activities will be seriously harmed. Economic dis-

location, unemployment, and a lower standard of living throughout the nation are likely to result.

Most people are appalled by the whole notion of this kind of international intrusion. However, proponents of the treaty feel quite the opposite, with many advocates holding the belief that Americans are far too excessive in their consumption and are responsible for many of the ecological problems around the globe. In fact, the American consumer is the subject of criticism in the Global Biodiversity Assessment itself. U.S. consumption habits are described in the documentation as "unsustainable," but a remedy is proposed.[68] Consumers can agree to cooperate with a global plan to drastically reduce world population, lowering it to less than half of its current total, or they can choose the regressive route and opt for the austere, agrarian lifestyle. A majority of Americans are unlikely to find either of these choices appealing or even remotely consistent with our guaranteed liberties.

The Man and Biosphere Program provides another glaring illustration of how circumvention of the ratification process through executive orders works. The United Nations created the Man and Biosphere Program[69] in 1971. This program is an international initiative that was designed to facilitate the implementation of the Biodiversity Treaty. In an effort to support the Man and Biosphere Program, in January of 1996 President Clinton issued Executive Order 12986,[70] which was designed to protect the International Union for Conservation of Nature and Natural Resources (IUCNNR) from future lawsuits. This group was afforded special treatment and granted immunity from lawsuits, a privilege usually reserved only for foreign diplomats. IUCNNR was given exceptional handling because it played an essential role in the creation and promotion of the Man and Biosphere Program. President Clinton, in conjunction with the State Department, proceeded to fulfill some of the goals of the Man and Biosphere Program, using executive orders and memoranda to bypass the normal legislative channels.[71]

Implementation of the Man and Biosphere Program is apparently a prerequisite to achieving the aims of the Biodiversity Treaty, as revealed in the documents of UNESCO. Commissions, whose members are selected from public and private organizations, govern the Man and Biosphere Program, in a similar arrangement to the bureaucracy of the GBA. These commissions are not elected, nor are they in any way accountable to the general public. Of course, the usual environmental non-governmental organizations (NGOs) are deeply involved in the operations.

The groundwork for the realization of the goals presented in the unratified Biodiversity Treaty has already been laid. The Man and Biosphere Program has been designating core areas deemed in need of protection. In fact, forty-seven large parcels, comprising a land mass greater than the state of Wyoming,[72] have already been placed under the UN banner by the Clinton administration. The principles of the GBA are guiding policy making at the Department of Interior and the Environmental Protection Agency as well. To further the goals of the GBA, the United States is being divided into twenty-one bioregions. It appears that the ultimate aim is to eradicate county and state boundaries and replace them with bioregional borders.

International treaties are being used to restrict the use of and access to these select areas. They are also being utilized to gain control of privately owned property located around these sites. If things proceed on the present course, in the not so distant future, property owners will be startled to find out that their rights have been completely altered by new land use regulations, and they will have had no prior warning or representative voice in the proceedings.

Globalism Advances

On 10 December 1998, with the nation's attention steadily focused upon the historical impeachment proceedings, President Clinton quietly signed Executive Order 13107, entitled "Implementation of Human Rights Treaties." This benign sounding designation does not begin to reveal the true potential for abuse that is contained within the provisions of the document. This executive order speaks not only of ratified treaties, but of "other relevant treaties . . . ," and sets up as the official policy of the United States government, the implementation of unapproved international treaties. It creates something called an Interagency Working Group, chaired by a designee of the Assistant to the President for National Security Affairs, to conduct the following functions, among others: (a) oversee legislation proposed by the administration to make certain that it is in conformity with UN human rights initiatives; (b) pursue public "education" slanted toward acceptance of UN initiatives; (c) design new methods of monitoring for the purposes of human rights obligations.

It may not be accidental that this executive order was signed at a time when the country was duly distracted and in the midst of a congressional transition. These factors would make it less likely that Congress would be able to disapprove the executive order during the thirty-day period that is required in order to prevent it from becoming law.

Sadly, it is quite possible that the "Implementation of Human Rights Treaties" will enable various unapproved UN treaties to take effect, wholly or in part, without the mandatory approval of the Senate. If this occurs, our national sovereignty will, once again, experience further erosion to the detriment of our autonomy and liberty.

Conclusion

The use of executive orders has mushroomed far beyond the boundaries initially assigned to the executive branch, but we must bear in mind that no governmental condition is static. Most of the basic protections that our forefathers built into the original framework still remain intact, and a noble, informed, and determined people can successfully reverse the pernicious trend that exists. But in order to reach the ultimate destination of a restored and balanced system, certain goals must be established.

First, information about these governmental instruments of power must be revealed and disseminated so that all Americans are grounded in the truth. The United States is not just another segment of the global body politic. Rather, it is a divinely inspired and sanctified archetype that is truly unequaled in the world. Its uniqueness must not be lost in the emerging tide of collectively acceptable misinformation. As a principled people, we must individually accept the mantle and do our part to preserve this unrivaled model of liberty. This entails warning our fellow citizens of the dangers that treaties and executive orders pose to the country and our cherished way of life. The public needs to fully understand that the threat is coming, not merely from outside our borders, but from the illegitimate use of executive orders as well.

Second, we must support and elect representatives at all levels of government who follow the principles of the Constitution. A good example of the type of representation that is needed is seen in Congresswoman Helen Chenoweth. She correctly noted the necessity to view executive orders in much the same way that we regard treaties, and she has worked to pass legislation to ensure that "the Constitution is the highest law of the land . . . rising above the executive orders and treaties."[73]

Ron Paul is another prototype member of Congress who will not vote for proposed legislation unless it is specifically authorized by the Constitution. As concerned and active citizens, we must involve ourselves in the election process at the grassroots level. Candidates must be asked directly whether they understand and intend to implement the actions necessary to reinstate the principles that the Constitution dictates, and, once elected, we must hold their feet to the fire and insist that they do.

Third, executive orders that encroach on the legislative process must be eliminated. Just as they came into being, slowly and incrementally, the offending executive orders must be removed from the law. This can be accomplished through congressional action and through the acts of a future president with a patriotic mindset. The American people must make this objective a priority and continue to monitor progress until it reaches fruition.

Fourth, we must value and protect our sovereignty. Those individuals who seek to promote an international agenda wish to use treaties and executive orders to undermine our national sovereignty. They view the United States as an obstacle to a homogeneous world assemblage. Just as our freedoms cannot be maintained without constant vigilance, our country's identity and singular national character cannot survive without steadfast guardianship.

Finally, we must restore the guiding principles for which our founding fathers courageously fought. The history and writings that gave birth to this nation have been removed from much of our public discussion. An anti-American curriculum has been promulgated in many of our schools. Religious expressions and traditions have been banished from town squares across our land. There has been a long, continuous chipping away of the founders' precepts.

The venerable idea that the law stands above the whims of any monarch, beyond political maneuvers, and superior to the government itself, is the essence of the founding fathers' vision. It is when this notion is honorably restored, when the dim fog is lifted from our aggregate blurred memory, that America will, once again, proceed down that familiar thoroughfare toward its resplendent destiny.

Appendix A
Executive Order 13083 "Federalism"

THE WHITE HOUSE
Office of the Press Secretary
(Birmingham, England)

For Immediate Release   May 14, 1998

EXECUTIVE ORDER

FEDERALISM

By the authority vested in me as President by the Constitution and the laws of the United States of America, and in order to guarantee the division of governmental responsibilities, embodied in the Constitution, between the Federal Government and the States that was intended by the Framers and application of those principles by the Executive departments and agencies in the formulation and implementation of policies, it is hereby ordered as follows:

Section 1. Definitions. For purposes of this order:

(a) "State" or "States" refer to the States of the United States of America, individually or collectively, and, where relevant, to State governments, including units of local government and other political subdivisions established by the States.

(b) "Policies that have federalism implications" refers to Federal regulations, proposed legislation, and other policy statements or actions that have substantial direct effects on the States or on the relationship, or the distribution of power and responsibilities, between the Federal Government and the States.

(c) "Agency" means any authority of the United States that is an "agency" under 44 U.S.C. 3502(1), other than those considered to be independent regulatory agencies, as defined in 44 U.S.C. 3502(5).

Sec. 2. Fundamental Federalism Principles. In formulating and implementing policies that have federalism implications, agencies shall be guided by the following fundamental federalism principles:

(a) The structure of government established by the Constitution is premised upon a system of checks and balances.

(b) The Constitution created a Federal Government of supreme, but limited, powers. The sovereign powers not granted to the Federal Government are reserved to the people or to the States, unless prohibited to the States by the Constitution.

(c) Federalism reflects the principle that dividing power between the Federal Government and the States serves to protect individual liberty. Preserving State authority provides an essential balance to the power of the Federal Government, while preserving the supremacy of Federal law provides an essential balance to the power of the States.

(d) The people of the States are at liberty, subject only to the limitations in the Constitution itself or in Federal law, to define the moral, political, and legal character of their lives.

(e) Our constitutional system encourages a healthy diversity in the public policies adopted by the people of the several States according to their own conditions, needs, and desires. States and local governments are often uniquely situated to discern the sentiments of the people and to govern accordingly.

(f) Effective public policy is often achieved when there is competition among the several States in the fashioning of different approaches to public policy issues. The search for enlightened public policy is often furthered when individual States and local governments are free to experiment with a variety of approaches to public issues. Uniform, national approaches to public policy problems can inhibit the creation of effective solutions to those problems.

(g) Policies of the Federal Government should recognize the responsibility of—and should encourage opportunities for—States, local governments, private associations, neighborhoods, families, and individuals to achieve personal, social, environmental, and economic objectives through cooperative effort.

Sec. 3. Federalism Policymaking Criteria. In addition to adhering to the fundamental federalism principles set forth in section 2 of this order, agencies shall adhere, to the extent permitted by law, to the following criteria when formulating and implementing policies that have federalism implications:

(a) There should be strict adherence to constitutional principles. Agencies should closely examine the constitutional and statutory authority supporting any Federal action that would limit the policymaking discretion of States and local governments, and should carefully assess the necessity for such action.

(b) Agencies may limit the policymaking discretion of States and local governments only after determining that there is constitutional and legal authority for the action.

(c) With respect to Federal statutes and regulations administered by States and local governments, the Federal Government should grant States and local governments the maximum administrative discretion possible. Any Federal oversight of such State and local administration should not unnecessarily intrude on State and local discretion.

(d) It is important to recognize the distinction between matters of national or multi-state scope (which may justify Federal action) and matters that are merely common to the States (which may not justify Federal action because individual States, acting individually or together, may effectively deal with them). Matters of national or multi-state scope that justify Federal action may arise in a variety of circumstances, including:

(1) When the matter to be addressed by Federal action occurs interstate as opposed to being contained within one State's boundaries.

(2) When the source of the matter to be addressed occurs in a State different from the State (or States) where a significant amount of the harm occurs.

(3) When there is a need for uniform national standards.

(4) When decentralization increases the costs of government thus imposing additional burdens on the taxpayer.

(5) When States have not adequately protected individual rights and liberties.

(6) When States would be reluctant to impose necessary regulations because of fears that regulated business activity will relocate to other States.

(7) When placing regulatory authority at the State or local level would undermine regulatory goals because high costs or demands for specialized expertise will effectively place the regulatory matter beyond the resources of State authorities.

(8) When the matter relates to Federally owned or managed property or natural resources, trust obligations, or international obligations.

(9) When the matter to be regulated significantly or uniquely affects Indian tribal governments.

Sec. 4. Consultation.

(a) Each agency shall have an effective process to permit elected officials and other representatives of State and local governments to provide meaningful and timely input in the development of regulatory policies that have federalism implications.

(b) To the extent practicable and permitted by law, no agency shall promulgate any regulation that is not required by statute, that has federalism implications, and that imposes substantial direct compliance costs on States and local governments, unless:

(1) funds necessary to pay the direct costs incurred by the State or local government in complying with the regulation are provided by the Federal Government; or

(2) the agency, prior to the formal promulgation of the regulation,

(A) in a separately identified portion of the preamble to the regulation as it is to be issued in the Federal Register, provides to the Director of the Office of Management and Budget a description of the extent of the agency's prior consultation with representatives of affected States and local governments, a summary of the nature of their concerns, and the agency's position supporting the need to issue the regulation; and

(B) makes available to the Director of the Office of Management and Budget any written communications submitted to the agency by States or local governments.

Sec. 5. Increasing Flexibility for State and Local Waivers.

(a) Agencies shall review the processes under which States and local governments apply for waivers of statutory and regulatory requirements and take appropriate steps to streamline those processes.

(b) Each agency shall, to the extent practicable and permitted by law, consider any application by a State or local government for a waiver of statutory or regulatory requirements in connection with any program administered by that agency with a general view toward increasing opportunities for utilizing flexible policy approaches at the State or local level in cases in which the proposed waiver is consistent with applicable Federal policy objectives and is otherwise appropriate.

(c) Each agency shall, to the extent practicable and permitted by law, render a decision upon a complete application for a waiver within 120 days of receipt of such application by the agency. If the application for a waiver is not granted, the agency shall provide the applicant with timely written notice of the decision and the reasons therefore.

(d) This section applies only to statutory or regulatory requirements that are discretionary and subject to waiver by the agency.

Sec. 6. Independent Agencies. Independent regulatory agencies are encouraged to comply with the provisions of this order.

Sec. 7. General Provisions.

(a) This order is intended only to improve the internal management of the executive branch and is not intended to, and does not, create any right or benefit, substantive or procedural, enforceable at law or equity by a party against the United States, its agencies or instrumentalities, its officers or employees, or any other person.

(b) This order shall supplement but not supersede the requirements contained in Executive Order 12866 ("Regulatory Planning and Review"), Executive Order 12988 ("Civil Justice Reform"), and OMB Circular A-19.

(c) Executive Order 12612 of October 26, 1987, and Executive Order 12875 of October 26, 1993, are revoked.

(d) The consultation and waiver provisions in sections 4 and 5 of this order shall complement the Executive order entitled, "Consultation and Coordination with Indian Tribal Governments," being issued on this day.

(e) This order shall be effective 90 days after the date of this order.

WILLIAM J. CLINTON
THE WHITE HOUSE,
May 14, 1998.

Executive Order 13095—Suspension of Executive Order 13083

By the authority vested in me as President by the Constitution and the laws of the United States of America and in order to enable full and adequate consultation with State and local elected officials, their representative organizations, and other interested parties, it is hereby ordered that Executive Order 13083, entitled "Federalism," is suspended.

WILLIAM J. CLINTON
THE WHITE HOUSE,
August 5, 1998.

Appendix B
Executive Order 13107
"Implementation of Human Rights Treaties"

THE WHITE HOUSE
Office of the Press Secretary

For Immediate Release   December 10, 1998

EXECUTIVE ORDER

IMPLEMENTATION OF HUMAN RIGHTS TREATIES

By the authority vested in me as President by the Constitution and the laws of the United States of America, and bearing in mind the obligations of the United States pursuant to the International Covenant on Civil and Political Rights (ICCPR), the Convention Against Torture and Other Cruel, Inhuman or Degrading Treatment or Punishment (CAT), the Convention on the Elimination of All Forms of Racial Discrimination (CERD), and other relevant treaties concerned with the protection and promotion of human rights to which the United States is now or may become a party in the future, it is hereby ordered as follows:

Section 1. Implementation of Human Rights Obligations.

(a) It shall be the policy and practice of the Government of the United States, being committed to the protection and promotion of human rights and fundamental freedoms, fully to respect and implement its obligations under the international human rights treaties to which it is a party, including the ICCPR, the CAT, and the CERD.

(b) It shall also be the policy and practice of the Government of the United States to promote respect for international human rights, both in our relationships with all other countries and by working with and strengthening the various international mechanisms for the promotion of human rights, including, inter alia, those of the United Nations, the International Labor Organization, and the Organization of American States.

Sec. 2. Responsibility of Executive Departments and Agencies.

(a) All executive departments and agencies (as defined in 5 U.S.C. 101-105, including boards and commissions, and hereinafter referred to collectively as "agency" or "agencies") shall maintain a current awareness of United States international human rights obligations that are relevant to their functions and shall perform such functions so as to respect and implement those obligations fully. The head of each agency shall designate a single contact officer who will be responsible for overall coordination of the implementation of this order. Under this order, all such agencies shall retain their established institutional roles in the implementation, interpretation, and enforcement of Federal law and policy.

(b) The heads of agencies shall have lead responsibility, in coordination with other appropriate agencies, for questions concerning implementation of human rights obligations that fall within their respective operating and program responsibilities and authorities or, to the extent that matters do not fall within the operating and program responsibilities and authorities of any agency, that most closely relate to their general areas of concern.

Sec. 3. Human Rights Inquiries and Complaints.

Each agency shall take lead responsibility, in coordination with other appropriate agencies, for responding to inquiries, requests for information, and complaints about violations of human rights obligations that fall within its areas of responsibility or, if the matter does not fall within its areas of responsibility, referring it to the appropriate agency for response.

Sec. 4. Interagency Working Group on Human Rights Treaties.

(a) There is hereby established an Interagency Working Group on Human Rights Treaties for the purpose of providing guidance, oversight, and coordination with respect to questions concerning the adherence to and implementation of human rights obligations and related matters.

(b) The designee of the Assistant to the President for National Security Affairs shall chair the Interagency Working Group, which shall consist of appropriate policy and legal representatives at the Assistant Secretary level from the Department of State, the Department of Justice, the Department of Labor, the Department of Defense, the Joint Chiefs of Staff, and other agencies as the chair deems appropriate. The principal members may designate alternates to attend meetings in their stead.

(c) The principal functions of the Interagency Working Group shall include:

(i) coordinating the interagency review of any significant issues concerning the implementation of this order and analysis and recommendations in connection with pursuing the ratification of human rights treaties, as such questions may from time to time arise;

(ii) coordinating the preparation of reports that are to be submitted by the United States in fulfillment of treaty obligations;

(iii) coordinating the responses of the United States Government to complaints against it concerning alleged human rights violations submitted to the United Nations, the Organization of American States, and other international organizations;

(iv) developing effective mechanisms to ensure that legislation proposed by the Administration is reviewed for conformity with international human rights obligations and that these obligations are taken into account in reviewing legislation under consideration by the Congress as well;

(v) developing recommended proposals and mechanisms for improving the monitoring of the actions by the various States, Commonwealths, and territories of the United States and, where appropriate, of Native Americans and Federally recognized Indian tribes, including the review of State, Commonwealth, and territorial laws for their conformity with relevant treaties, the provision of relevant information for reports and other monitoring purposes, and the promotion of effective remedial mechanisms;

(vi) developing plans for public outreach and education concerning the provisions of the ICCPR, CAT, CERD, and other relevant treaties, and human rights-related provisions of domestic law;

(vii) coordinating and directing an annual review of United States reservations, declarations, and understandings to human rights treaties, and matters as to which there have been non-trivial complaints or allegations of inconsistency with or breach of international human rights obligations, in order to determine whether there should be consideration of any modification of relevant reservations, declarations, and understandings to human rights treaties, or United States practices or laws. The results and recommendations of this review shall be reviewed by the head of each participating agency;

(viii) making such other recommendations as it shall deem appropriate to the President, through the Assistant to the President for National Security Affairs, concerning United States adherence to or implementation of human rights treaties and related matters; and

(ix) coordinating such other significant tasks in connection with human rights treaties or international human rights institutions, including the Inter-American Commission on Human Rights and the Special Rapporteurs and complaints procedures established by the United Nations Human Rights Commission.

(d) The work of the Interagency Working Group shall not supplant the work of other interagency entities, including the President's Committee on the International Labor Organization, that address international human rights issues.

Sec. 5. Cooperation Among Executive Departments and Agencies.

All agencies shall cooperate in carrying out the provisions of this order. The Interagency Working Group shall facilitate such cooperative measures.

Sec. 6. Judicial Review, Scope, and Administration.

(a) Nothing in this order shall create any right or benefit, substantive or procedural, enforceable by any party against the United States, its agencies or instrumentalities, its officers or employees, or any other person.

(b) This order does not supersede Federal statutes and does not impose any justiciable obligations on the executive branch.

(c) The term "treaty obligations" shall mean treaty obligations as approved by the Senate pursuant to Article II, section 2, clause 2 of the United States Constitution.

(d) To the maximum extent practicable and subject to the availability of appropriations, agencies shall carry out the provisions of this order.

WILLIAM J. CLINTON
THE WHITE HOUSE,
December 10, 1998.

Appendix C
How to Research Executive Orders

Executive Orders from 1936 to the present are available from the *Federal Register*. The *Federal Register* can be found at approximately 1,400 federal depository libraries throughout the United States and its territories, with at least one library situated in almost every Congressional district. Federal depository libraries can also be accessed on the internet at http://www.access.gpo.gov/su_docs/dpos/adpos003.html. In addition, information may be obtained by contacting the Government Printing Office user support service at 1-888-293-6498.

Executive orders and proclamations are published in various resources according to the year of execution.

1789-1983
Cis Index to Presidential Executive Orders and Proclamations. KF70.A55C561987

1791-
United States Statutes at Large. (Proclamations only) KF 50 U5

1929-1933
Herbert Hoover: Proclamations and Executive Orders, March 4, 1929, to March 4, 1933. GS4.113/2:H76

1936-

Code of Federal Regulations. 3, President. (Annual) 1936-. KF 70 A34 C64 INTERNET: http://www.gpo.ucop.edu/search/cfr.html

Federal Register. KF 70 A2 (Latest 2 years) INTERNET: http://www.gpo.ucop.edu/search/fedfld.html (1994-.)

1945-

Codification of Presidential Proclamations and Executive Orders, April 13, 1945, to January 20, 1989. AE 2.113

1965-

Weekly Compilation of Presidential Documents. (Weekly) 1965-. AE 2.109

United States Code Annotated. (Annual) KF 70 A34 C64
INTERNET: http://www.gpo.ucop.edu/search/uscode.html

Other internet resources:

• JFK Executive Orders
http://www.lib.umich.edu/libhome/Documents.center/jfkeo.html

• White House Search of Executive Orders: 1993-2001
http://www.pub.whitehouse.gov/search/executive-orders.html

• Presidential Executive Orders, 1993 to present Executive Order Disposition Tables, 1961+
http://www.nara.gov/fedreg/eo.html

• Weekly Compilation of Presidential Documents, 1993+
http://www.access.gpo.gov/nara/nara003.html

• Intelligence Documents (Federation of American Scientists) Executive Orders related to Intelligence Activities
http://www.fas.org/irp/offdocs.html

Notes

1. Statement by White House Communications Counsel Paul Begala as quoted by James Bennet in "Back from China, Clinton Focuses on Domestic Policy Events to Remind Voters of His Desire to Fix Problems Here at Home," *New York Times* (5 July 1998).

2. See "Executive Orders and Proclamations: A Study of a Use of Presidential Power," printed for the House Committee on Government Operations, 85th Congress, First Session, 37 (1957).

3. Theodore Roosevelt, *An Autobiography* (New York: Scribners, 1958), 197-200.

4. William Howard Taft, *Our Chief Magistrate and His Powers* (New York: Columbia University Press, 1916), 138-45.

5. House Committee on Government Operations, *Executive Orders and Proclamations,* 85th Congress First Session, December 1957, 36.

6. Alexis Simendinger, "Congress and Clinton Wage Paper War," *National Journal* (27 July 1998).

7. *Korematsu v. United States,* 323 U.S. 214.

8. 323 U.S. 214, 223.

9. 6 Fed. Reg. 2777 (1941).

10. Ibid.

11. *Youngstown Co. v. Sawyer,* 343 U.S. 579 (1952).

12. Ibid.

13. Ibid., 587.

14. Ibid., 589.

15. 64 Stat. 997 (1950). See *Communist Party of the United States v. SACB*, 367 U.S. 1 (1961).

16. E.O. 11605, 36 Fed. Reg. 12831 (1971). See *American Service Men's Union v. Mitchell*, 54 F.R.D. 14, 17 (D.D.C. 1972). Dicta in the case noted that a president could not delegate such power through Executive Orders.

17. Simendinger, *National Journal*.

18. Ibid.

19. E.O. 8802, 6 Fed. Reg. 3109 (1941); E.O. 10308, 16 Fed. Reg. 12303 (1951); E.O. 10479, 18 Fed. Reg. 4899 (1953); E.O. 10925, 26 Fed. Reg. 1977 (1961); E.O. 11246, 30 Fed. Reg. 12319 (1965).

20. *United States v. Eliason*, 41 U.S. 291, 301 (1842).

21. The Constitution of the United States, Article II.

22. Edward S. Corwin, *The President: Office and Powers, 1789-1957*, 4th ed. (New York: New York University Press, 1957).

23. *In re Neagle*, 135 U.S. 1 (1890).

24. *United States v. Nixon*, 418 U.S. 683, 706.

25. Arthur M. Schlesinger, Jr., *The Imperial Presidency* (New York: Popular Library, 1974), 324.

26. Executive Order 11652, 37 Fed. Reg. 5209 (1972).

27. *New York Times v. United States*, 403 U.S. 713.

28. Executive Order 12919, 59 Fed. Reg. 29525 (1994).

29. Executive Order 10995, 27 Fed. Reg. 1519 (1962).

30. Executive Order 10997, 27 Fed. Reg. 1522 (1962).

31. *Brown v. Burnstein,* D.C. Pa., 49 F. Supp. 728, 732.

32. Executive Order 10998, 27 Fed. Reg. 1524 (1962).

33. Executive Order 10999, 27 Fed. Reg. 1527 (1962).

34. Executive Order 11000, 27 Fed. Reg. 1532 (1962). Authority for this is reflected in Title 50 App. United States Code Sec. 2153, "War and National Defense."

35. Executive Order 12148, 44 Fed. Reg. 43239 (1979), signed by President Jimmy Carter. Executive Order 11051, 27 Fed. Reg. 9683 (1962), authorizes all of these executive orders into effect in times of national emergency.

36. Title 2 United States Code 5121 (Stafford Act).

37. Clinton Administration Policy on Reforming Multilateral Peace Operations (P.D.D. 25), U.S. Department of State Publication Number 10161, released by the Bureau of International Organization Affairs (May 1994). This document may be found at George Mason University. http://ralph.gmu.edu/cfpa/peace/pdd25.html.

38. The Combat Arms Survey was sent to Geoff Metcalf by a U.S. Marine. It was accompanied by a written explanation indicating that the survey was conducted at a Marine base in Twenty-nine Palms, California, on 10 May 1994.

39. Robert Pear, "Under Clinton, the Presidential Pen is Mightier than Ever," *New York Times* (28 June 1998).

40. Pear, *New York Times.*

41. Sandra Sobieraj, "Clinton to Refocus on U.S. Agenda," *Associated Press* (5 July 1998).

42. James Bennet, "Back from China, Clinton Focuses on Domestic Policy. Events to Remind Voters of His Desire to Fix Problems Here at Home," *New York Times* 5 July 1998).

43. Simendinger, *National Journal*.

44. Elizabeth Shogren, "President Plans Blitz of Executive Orders, Clinton Intent on Pressing Social Reforms," *Los Angeles Times* (3 July 1998).

45. Simendinger, *National Journal*.

46. Shogren, *Los Angeles Times*.

47. Ibid.

48. Adam D. Thierer, "President Clinton's Sell-Out of Federalism," *The Heritage Foundation* (25 June 1998).

49. United States Constitution, Bill of Rights, Tenth Amendment.

50. Executive Order 13083, 63 Fed. Reg. 27651 (1998), Section 3 (d) (3).

51. Ibid., Section 3 (d) (5).

52. Ibid., Section 3 (d) (6).

53. Thierer, *The Heritage Foundation*.

54. David S. Broder, "Executive Order Urged Consulting, But Didn't," *Washington Post* (16 July 1998).

55. Thierer, *The Heritage Foundation*.

56. "Clinton Suspends Federalism Order," *The Associated Press* (5 August 1998).

57. Paul Shepard, "Clinton Seeks New Federalism Policy," *Associated Press* (17 August 1998).

58. Ibid.

59. American Heritage Rivers Initiative. http:// www.amrivers.org.

60. Robert Burns, "Clinton Designates U.S. Waterways," *Associated Press* (30 July 1998).

61. "Federal River Grab Coming Next Week: 'Heritage' Initiative to Give U.S. More Land Control," *WorldNetDaily* (21 January 1998). http//www.worldnetdaily.com. See also Phyllis Schlafly, "Clinton Is Selling Us down the Rivers," (4 March 1998). http:// www.eagleforum.org/column/1998/mar98/98-03-04.html.

62. Keith Russell, "Stroke of His Pen Subverts the Law," *Insight Magazine* (27 July 1998).

63. Ibid.

64. See James Hirsen, *The Coming Collision: Global Law vs. U.S. Liberties* (Lafayette, LA: Huntington House, 1999).

65. V.H. Heywood, ed., *Global Biodiversity Assessment* (New York: Cambridge University Press, 1996).

66. Ibid.

67. Ibid., Section 10.5.

68. Ibid., Section 9.

69. UNESCO Man and Biosphere Program Home Page. http://www.unesco.org/mab/themabnet.htm.

70. Executive Order 12986, 61 Fed. Reg. 1693 (1996).

71. U.S. Man and Biosphere Program Home Page. http://www.mabnetamericas.org/home2.html.

72. Natural Resources Defense Council, *What is a Biosphere Reserve?* http://mail.igc.apc.org/nrdc/bkgrd/fobio.html.

73. Representative Chenoweth believes we need to res-
urrect the Bricker Amendment to make sure that executive orders and treaties never supersede the Constitution. See James Hirsen, *The Coming Collision: Global
Law vs. U.S. Liberties* (Lafayette, LA: Huntington
House, 1999).